Going Forward

Also by Cynthia Hallam and published by Ginninderra Press
Bread and Butter People
Rising to the Occasion
Town Life
Living in the Moment
Moving with the Times
New Horizons
Here and Now
Life Happens
Onwards and Upwards

Cynthia Hallam

Going Forward

Acknowledgements

As always, my heartfelt thanks to my daughter Trish de Jong
for her unfailing encouragement and thoughtful editing,
Warren Nicholls for his inspiring stewardship of our writing group
and Stephen Matthews OAM for his ongoing faith in my poetic
aspirations.

For Trish and Peter,
Michael and Ben
with all my love

Going Forward
ISBN 978 1 76109 668 6
Copyright © text Cynthis Hallam 2024
Cover image: Trish de Jong

First published 2024 by
GINNINDERRA PRESS
PO Box 3461 Port Adelaide 5015
www.ginninderrapress.com.au

Contents

On Going Forward	7
Fantasy	8
Suburbia	9
A Doggy Perspective	10
The Aspects of Love	11
Opportunity	12
Acquiescence	13
Ambience	14
Delicious!	15
Swinging	16
Another One	17
An Illuminating Experience	18
Fate's Chances	19
Creatures Great and Small	20
Rumination	21
A Major Operation	22
Weathering the Weather	23
Modern Lives	24
Traffic Lights	25
A Brief Encounter	26
Nature's Promise	27
Intermission	28
Weeding	29
Compromise	30
An Accidental Observation	31
Inspiration	32
Chilly Prospects	33
A Matter of Perception	34
A Feeling of Goodwill	35
Dreams	36

Satisfaction	37
Diving into the Gene Pool	38
Small Pleasures	39
A Shopping Dissertation	40
Impressions	41
Aggravation	42
The Business of Success	43
Conviviality	44
Expectation	45
Puzzlers	46
Saving the Planet	47
Disaster	48
A Little Escape	49
Inking	50
Go Team!	51
Whose Town is it?	52
Distraction	53
Joy	54
Commercialism	55
The Hirsute Pursuit	56
The Gambler	57
Garbage	58
Milk	59
Ouch!	60

On Going Forward

Her mind was finally made up.
With world peace uncertain,
climate off-kilter, virus rampant
and disrupting dissent rising,
personal connections seemed
more important than ever
and coping with life on her own
had now brought this home.
So, with her well-being at stake,
she has devised a radical plan
and drops invites in letter boxes
all along her street
to bring a chair to her address
at two o'clock on Saturday
for a neighbourhood gathering.

But just as failure is conceded
for no one has shown up,
the woman who walks her dog
several times a day arrives,
followed by three more singles
then two elderly couples
and after an awkward start,
names and opinions exchange,
conversations blossom
as garden advice is offered
and as interaction grows,
she hopes that any loneliness
is being assuaged like hers,
by a new feeling of belonging.

Fantasy

It is an early spring Saturday afternoon
and here in our local park
a birthday celebration is in full swing.
Pink balloons hang from a leafy branch
above a table full of festive treats
and a cake adorned with five candles.

A cluster of excited children
are enjoying a game guided by a Mum
in a floating dress and wings,
oblivious to the amused observation
of those passing by, and like me,
are being utterly charmed
by the delightfully innocent scenario,
happy that one childhood tradition
is still remaining alive and well
despite the challenges of the times.

Suburbia

To my surprise, an agent's 'To Let' sign
is on display in the house's front yard,
newest tenants seemingly just moved in,
and remember that over the years,
there had been a plethora of occupants
residing at this particular address.

On my daily exercise around the block,
there've been times when the place
has attracted my closer attention.
Twice, ambulances were parked outside
and once a police car in the drive.
Balloons have floated over the letter box
on other obviously, happy occasions,
but the speed of this event is a mystery.
Had the rent not been forthcoming?
Did Dad's job just get transferred
or perhaps he has just been put in jail
and the family now living with relatives.

However, looking on the bright side,
maybe the lease had simply been short
and nothing dramatic ever happened
behind this nondescript façade,
but at least my walk will be enlivened
by some more wild speculation.

A Doggy Perspective

I am pruning shrubs around the letter box
as another resident of our street arrives
and pauses to have a bit of a natter
before continuing on her afternoon walk
over to the park
with her friendly old Labradoodle.

The entrenched animal lover that I am,
I say hello to her curly canine companion
who extends his paw to be shaken,
and the charmer that he is, I can't resist
so happily oblige
and a wagging tail reciprocates.

After the usual discussion of local affairs
and the current capricious weather,
the impatient dog strains on his leash
to sniff weemails on the telegraph pole
and sends a reply,
then both are ready to move on.

The Aspects of Love

They say it makes the world go around
but is expressed in so many ways.
The feelings for partners and family,
a devotion to God or other deity.
Ardour for reckless games, activities,
or more cerebral interests.
Passion for some foods or beverages,
even tenderness for an adored pet,
yet all susceptible to dislocation
by circumstances beyond our control.

But ultimately, in our life's tapestry,
regardless of any transience,
it is a vital element of our well-being
and the most satisfying by far,
so as a dear friend and mentor
always avowed, 'LONG LIVE LOVE!'

Opportunity

The evening news has just reported
that a public Christmas tree has been set alight
by a homeless man, desperate enough
to commit a totally visible crime,
believing that a roof over his head even in gaol
during the cold, European winter weather
was preferable to his current dismal situation
and as I partake of my own evening meal
in the comfort of my home here in Australia,
I ponder the alarming division
between the haves and have nots everywhere
that seems to be growing wider each day,
heightened by the current rampaging viruses,
and resolve to be more appreciative
of my own relatively normal life down under.

Acquiescence

A brand-new year has just begun so this morning,
the Christmas decorations were packed up
but the house is looking so bare
without the annual, visible signs of festivities
and I can't help wondering what the embryo year
has got in store for us.

Will it evolve into some designated 'new normal'
to which we all must grow accustomed?
Will some amazing new invention excite us?
May space travel become a viable holiday option?
A major health issue find a miraculous cure?
Climate change slow down to a sustainable level
or even world peace?

Ah well, perhaps it is pointless predicting a future
which as always, will travel its own path,
be subject to events I can do nothing about
so just relax in front of the telly with a cup of tea
and enjoy the cricket.

Ambience

It is supposed to be our high summer
but La Niña has hijacked the sun
then substituted a fine drizzle
and periods of enervating humidity.
Instead of fluttering on lines outside,
washing is hanging on verandas
over saturated shoes and umbrellas.

Rampant weeds are all running riot
in these perfect, dank conditions
but much too often in the dry spells,
an unexpected unseasonal chill
renders any gardening unpleasant.

But at least, in our own location,
earthquakes aren't wreaking havoc,
tornados not flattening homes
or snowstorms paralysing activity
so with no way of controlling it,
must take the weather in our stride
and complaints in a new direction.

Delicious!

It is the mango season again
and one of our great pleasures
is eating this luscious fruit.
But no matter how carefully
the whole situation is handled,
sticky juice will still dribble
over chins and down our arms.

Whether basic peel and munch,
lateral cut or neatly diced slice
it makes no difference
how the process is approached,
and using a spoon to scoop up
this manna from heaven
would be an absolute sacrilege.

But afterwards, the clean up
is always a willing price to pay
for providing us time to reflect
on the gastronomic joy
that we have just experienced.
To savour it all over again,
our tastebuds still wallowing.

Swinging

The children's playground in the park
is being well patronised today,
most of the equipment being enjoyed
by youngsters on school holidays
and toddlers eager to be experiencing
their first attempts at daring-do.
I notice that one swing is now vacant
and resist the desire to have a go
in case the authorities might be called
to take this weirdo into care.

But thoughts persist of former times
in the backyard of my youth
when in a relaxed, meditative mood,
I would swing back and forth
under the huge camphor laurel
seeking inspiration for a composition
almost due, which surprisingly,
more often than not usually worked,
and even the memory of it
has prompted this contemplation.

Another One

Well, here we go again,
allegations of infamy
against a public figure.
Where will it end?
Anyone can be accused
of anything at all,
still in progression
or in their earlier lives,
although it may be
absolutely unfounded
and merely a rumour.

No matter how famed
the chosen target,
(and even the Royals
are not immune,}
if it makes a newscast
or current affairs
the initiator wins.
Validity may implode
at a future time,
but current damage
remembered forever.

An Illuminating Experience

In the endless, clear and star-studded sky,
a radiantly glowing full moon is hovering
and I wonder if any covert lunar aliens
are observing earth's legion of peccadillos.
The dissatisfaction, avarice, chicanery,
selfish disregard for any other's interests.
The possessive rivalry between nations
motivating the race to claim their home.

Somehow, the luminescence encourages
reflection within its tranquil ambience.
Imagining the nature of a perfect world.
Dreaming of a peaceful, utopian existence
that I envisage could one day eventuate.
Wave to assure any up there watching
that I am not a lunatic in the classic sense.
Just grateful to be sharing the moonlight.

Fate's Chances

Have you ever given any thought
that as most days proceed as usual,
some will remain in our memories
for turning out so incredibly well
or frustratingly, so utterly wrong
from the time you have woken up.

After a welcome, refreshing sleep,
there is a rare, relaxed breakfast,
the kids are being absolute angels
so enjoy a bit of time to yourself.
Have a lovely chat with a friend,
the rain eases up for the playdate
and kids' bedtime is drama-free.

Then there are disastrous days
as toast made from the last slices
in the bread tin has incinerated.
An unpredicted storm sweeps in
as you start pegging out washing
and a monumental traffic snarl
delays all of your best laid plans.

Whether working, now retired
or living a self-styled existence,
we cannot forever guarantee
the progress of usual lifestyles
so any single, preordained path
not always our future destiny.

Creatures Great and Small

In the kitchen, she automatically stepped forward
and stomped on the ant scurrying over the floor
as she made herself a cup of tea before sitting down
to watch another David Attenborough naturefest.
An inveterate advocate for all living creatures,
as she observed insect life in an Amazonian forest
it suddenly occurred to her what she had just done,
by brutally taking the life of that poor little ant.

She had a sudden, unnerving attack of 'what ifs?'
Was it on its way back to its nest with sustenance
for a hungry family that is anxiously waiting
and leaving them abandoned to starve to death?
Had she just wantonly murdered for no reason?
Upset the universe's delicate ecological balance?

What if the proverbial boot was on the other foot
and giant marsupials invaded from outer space
then tramped on humans as if we were worthless,
determined to destroy us for their own comfort?
Sipping her tea did nothing to assuage her guilt
so vowed to have more regard for all other beings.
Swatted the mosquito that landed on her arm
and turned her full attention back to the Amazon.

Rumination

In the light of a new day,
somehow, everything seems a bit different.
During the previous dark evening hours,
current problems may have seemed insurmountable
but now, after giving it some thought,
a tiny glimpse of possibility may start filtering in
with that first eye-opening steaming cup,
and while all difficulties can't be miraculously solved
by the advent of daylight's benign ambience,
perhaps a firmer resolve to persevere can arise
to help assuage any feelings of despair
and settle down any pestering, lingering doubts.
Encourage a more positive confidence in the future.
Well, in theory anyway!

A Major Operation

She was in no way a financial tycoon
but with her bank term deposit renewal approaching,
she set about checking that her precious investment
would provide her with the best possible return.
She investigated and compared many other strategies.
Pondered safety aspects of opportunities elsewhere.
Even drafted her version of one of those spread sheets
she'd read about in the business section of the paper.

When reinvestment day finally arrived,
choice now irrevocably made, she entered her bank
with the confidence of a seasoned fiscal entrepreneur,
satisfied that their interest currently on offer
was the best way to entrust her ten thousand dollars.
In fact, may even have a sherry when she got home
to celebrate the success of her pecuniary perspicacity.
Being a monetary expert was draining, thirsty work!

Weathering the Weather

Lately, this master of surprise has been having a field day.
Rain one minute and then a sudden burst of sunshine
entices us outside to luxuriate in its welcome ambience
until from nowhere, a shower sneaks up behind our back
and for the umpteenth time, the need for dry apparel.
The dog restrained from shaking a saturated coat inside.

Is this much-reported climate change we are now facing
our own fault or the natural evolution of the universe?
Theories abound worldwide from verbose climatologists
and we all have our personal opinions on this matter
but regardless, must still remain mindful of the positives
for at least we have something handy to whinge about.

Modern Lives

No matter what the current conditions are,
for some, life can be besieged by uncertainty.
Livelihoods or possessions put in jeopardy
by a situation that was beyond their control
is forever clouding their entire future
with hosts of 'but what ifs', 'depending ons'
or decisions that it was not the right time,
even if their security is never in question
as occurs overseas in less blessed countries.

But propaganda and blatant misinformation
continues to filter into their subconscious
and to them, any freelance aspirations
or the natural progression of their dreams
can no longer promise eventual fruition
despite original confidence in the planning
so we can only hope they are also aware
the best way to bolster positive thinking
is that old mantra 'Take one day at a time.'

Traffic Lights

They can be a nuisance or saviour when out driving.
An annoying inconvenience if we are running late,
a blessing, when time is of the essence,
but with our road usage continuing to escalate,
a prayer should be offered for those back in the day
who surveyed prevailing population trends,
foreshadowed the expansion of a locality's mobility
and installed these bastions of the law.

Whether introduced before a coming state election
to inspire voters in the neighbourhood
or just the foresight to plan for the common good,
regardless of our day-to-day frustrations
or the angst we put ourselves through at the time,
our hearts and minds must honestly concede,
a life without those bossy ambers, reds and greens
would truly, be absolutely unthinkable.

A Brief Encounter

Looking out through the kitchen window,
movement within the foliage of the fruit tree
catches my eye
then notice the white feathers of a cockatoo
balancing on a slender, swaying branch
and vigorously pecking into a half-ripe lemon.

But then it severs the stem and lets it fall
while shuffling towards the next temptation
to be followed
again and again by this pointless routine
until I have to restrain myself from shouting
that each of them will just taste the same.

But intrigued now, I stay silent as I observe
until realising
I am witnessing an awful wanton waste,
go hurrying outside and send it on its way,
copping squawks of avian indignation
blasting my eardrums for the interruption.

Nature's Promise

After a wetter than usual summer,
the leaves seem reluctant to morph
into their habitual spectacular demise
even though the middle of autumn
is already just around the corner.

By now, deciduous trees should be
a massive blaze of glorious colour,
the saffrons, russets and vermilions
bursting forth into the magnificence
of a spectacular foliage farewell.

So, detecting some minor changes
in the maple trees out in the yard,
I'm relieved that the seasonal cycle
continues but has just been delayed
and Mother Nature has it sorted.

Intermission

A couple are strolling through the local park
and a lively collie bounds ahead of them,
turning often with a broad hairy grin
to make sure they are close and following.
The man launches a ball and eagerly,
it races off to retrieve it and drops it back
with the expectation of more to come
until checking her watch, the lady calls time.

The collie lifts its leg against a nearby pole
then all smiling, plus one wagging tail,
the contented little family returns to a car,
dusty with the detritus of country travel
and crammed to the roof with luggage,
to resume their journey towards the coast,
the stop off for a short, relaxing break
obviously a mutually satisfying experience.

Weeding

Regardless of the seasonal weather,
our gardening prowess
or any other relevant circumstance,
weeds still overcome all obstacles
to emerge and flourish in abundance.
Seemingly overnight,
green shoots can erupt from the soil
only recently confidently declared
to be free of any further infestations.

Winged and four-clawed residents
of the neighbourhood
seem to completely ignore them
in favour of plantings being nurtured
and it seems such a waste
of nature's own recycling capability
that they aren't tastier than parsley,
so if we are being totally realistic,
must stoically accept their incursion.

Compromise

In many facets of our lives, it is an ideal panacea
which can improve the nature of a relationship,
business operation or international encounter,
concept of working together for a common good
and a better understanding of another opinion
encouraging a confident feeling of achievement,
mutual appraisal and acceptance of difference
often engendering some interactive agreement
or an enduring friendship.

But naturally, there will always be those entities
for whom compromise is an unknown quality,
their own views the only ones they will tolerate,
see cooperation as an indication of weakness
and without shame promote their own agendas
so that all we can do if being majorly impacted
is be ready for any unexpected repercussions
if your conciliation options remain unresolved,
but of course, that's life!

An Accidental Observation

When you consider the millions of vehicles
plying our country's vast system of roads,
it is a tribute to the rule abiding nature
of the majority of our population
that the percentage of our misadventures
is such a gratifying, microscopic proportion
of what the tally actually could have been.

Drivers always have a reason for heading
to a chosen destination at any given time.
Deliveries from one location to another.
Picking up the kids from school.
Going into town to keep an appointment.
Motoring to a covert romantic rendezvous
or simply enjoying a pleasant holiday tour.

But no one ever plans to have an accident
causing harm, expense or inconvenience,
yet many chatter on hand-held phones
or exhibit a dearth of awareness
owing to some recent overindulgence,
each one unconsciously breaking the law
and naturally, would never apply to us!

Inspiration

The creative instinct is so utterly ephemeral.
Embryo ideas can be assailing our brains
from all directions, but when needed most,
have apparently retreated into obscurity
and become just one more distant promise.

The brilliant notion that was out of the blue
Is usually a vastly encouraging prospect,
but sometimes, you come to a realisation
it is very similar to another somewhere else.

So, if brainwaves appear to have atrophied,
something has to be done to motivate
the imagination that still remains behind
and enhance the likelihood of achievement.

But while any incentive is always welcome,
surely the most satisfying feeling of all
must be waking up grasping the concept
that frustratingly, had eluded you for days.

So one must hope that within our psyche,
the magic of inspiration is still lingering
in the deep recesses of our subconscious,
and will eventually, result in triumph.
Could even be a good subject for a poem!

Chilly Prospects

A precursor of winter has just arrived with a bang,
or actually, via the whoosh of a frigid, polar wind
that is creeping into each single bone in our body.
However, any vision of this season's discomfort
can be eased by the small pleasures it engenders.

The satisfaction as the warmth from your hands
wrapped around a mug of a favourite beverage
infiltrates then heartens your entire constitution.
The feeling of security when snuggled up inside
while an Antarctic trespasser is rattling windows.

Obviously, winter is welcomed by fervent skiers
and the footy season is nirvana for ardent fans.
Grass is going to sleep, the mower stored away
and weeds, so rampant over the humid autumn
seem to be declaring a truce for the time being.

Of course, less daylight has a few disadvantages
and the next power bill can be a bit of a shock.
Fog makes commuter driving rather hazardous
and the regular single-digit mornings a real trial,
but hey! At least we are over all that sweating!

A Matter of Perception

Time can elapse for us very swiftly or slowly,
depending on our current state of mind.
At any given stage throughout our existence,
many feel that they are speeding through life
with the days too short to accommodate it,
yet, if coping with depression or misfortune
find each twenty-four hours a constant drag.

It can seem endless to be waiting in a queue
if we are supposed to be somewhere else
but the same period passes by more quickly
if at the dentist prior to root canal therapy
and the prospect is now having to be faced.
The dinner date with a bore is plodding on
but racing if a new relationship is blooming.

So, it is not the regular, sixty-minute hours
that change their time frames at will,
just mood swings dictating their direction,
and should realise that time's progression
is an accurate indication of our well-being,
even when contentedly, we are ignoring it,
for unconsciously, its erudition is infallible.

A Feeling of Goodwill

On this sunny Saturday morning,
the shops as usual are booming.
A young couple ambles along,
the tired mother pushing a pram,
a toddler shepherded by his dad.
They pause by an upmarket car
parked in all its glory at the kerb,
and she waits while he dreams,
then ruefully laughing, move on,
and I realise how this streetscape
reflects the nature of our town.

The stoic acceptance of life as is
and coping with what it is not.
The lack of any vacant premises
a testimony to retail confidence
and knowledge of the customers.
An ingrained sense of belonging
as a passing casual connection
smiles then greets you by name
regardless of status difference.
Our life in this small community
a bonus for all who call it home.

Dreams

On waking up, I am usually at peace,
except after having had a nightmare
that somehow, stays in my memory,
relived in detail during the next day
despite having no personal relevance,
and not inspired by the night's news
or the plot of a current library book
so its genesis is a complete mystery
and sometimes, just won't go away.

I have no recall of any similar events
to prompt such a disturbing scenario
that is so foreign to my constitution
and rather have my mindset at ease,
not full of disturbing, bizarre images
usurping normal, rational thoughts,
but are thankfully, assuaged by time,
and hope of sweeter dreams ahead
a healing notion to look forward to.

Satisfaction

On arriving to purchase a few groceries,
she narrowly evades being sideswiped
by a driver backing out again from a park
to realign an upmarket four-wheel drive.
He opens his door with a stream of abuse
about all you so and so women drivers
who should never be allowed on the road
and shocked to receive his unfair tirade,
she carefully checks the clearance behind
and retreats to give him plenty of room
while his line up reaches perfection
then she moves to a vacant spot nearby.

But in the supermarket checkout queue,
she finds herself behind the same driver
and after having some serious thoughts,
concludes that she didn't have the nerve
to prod him in the back in retribution.
But after he has finished his transaction,
he turns to find out what is happening,
recognising who it is having a great laugh
at the toilet paper heaped in his trolley,
his discomfort very obvious as he leaves,
the upset he had previously inflicted
subsiding as she takes her turn at the till.

Diving into the Gene Pool

Every human who is currently living on this planet
bears the imprint of generations of antecedents
determining the progression of any previous traits,
the passing on of inherent health aberrations
or the ongoing style of our personal relationships
as we manage the vicissitudes of day-to-day living.

Naturally, our physical features are predetermined
by whoever is a part of our own particular lineage
as is strength of character, nobility of aspirations
or willingness to toil hard for desired results
but an attitude of idleness or an aversion to work
could mean an ancestor has plenty to answer for!

So the ability to effectively provide our livelihood
or a total disinclination to be breaking the law
may in the long run simply come down to genetics
and which tendencies remain firmly in the chain
or lost in time depends on this lineal gamble,
which in essence shapes the direction of our fate.

Small Pleasures

Keeping the bird bath topped up
has become a labour of love
when from a window,
I watch splashes of avian ablution
and others waiting in the wings
(no pun intended)
for their turn to start cooling off.

I am no longer surprised that
most mornings see a reduction
in the levels of the water,
happy that the resident possums
and other nocturnal wildlife
know of its location
and have taken their usual fill.

But I have no reason to complain
for with an animal loving bias,
I am forever in awe
of Mother Nature's expertise,
her gifts such a great distraction
from life's challenges
as I enjoy the delights on offer.

A Shopping Dissertation

With all the complexities of modern life,
a quick trip to pick up a few groceries
can sometimes disappear into the ether.
For an example, just look at today.
As well as acquiring the basic supplies,
I will obtain some cash from the ATM,
visit the RTA for the car registration,
post office to pay insurance and rates,
the chemist to have a prescription filled
then the library to change my books.

I will leave the food shopping until last
so the frozen peas will not defrost,
but first, I need to stop off for petrol
then search for a supermarket park.
I suppose these days, this is all routine
but will really welcome that cuppa
after I retrieve my bag of purchases
and with relief shut the garage door,
hoping that in sorting everything else
I haven't forgotten to get the milk!

Impressions

With no dog on a leash or phone clamped to my ear,
I feel quite out of place as I stroll through the park
on my daily afternoon constitutional.
Someone has just run by almost knocking me down,
probably heading for the station as a train is due,
but the inevitable phone is claiming all his attention.
Even the approaching young mum wheeling a pram
with no phone to her ear, has the baby's carriage
attached to the leash of a huge and enthusiastic dog.

I am fond of dogs and, in fact, all living creatures,
but, while happy to see them in obvious loving care,
feel no need to follow the current trend
for an excuse to take a walk in these different times,
using the quiet stroll to exercise underused limbs,
mull over anything needing some close attention
or simply pleasantly strolling with my mind at peace
but confess, my phone is always in my pocket
in case communication may be urgently required.

Aggravation

These days there's no escape from it.
After almost having to use a power drill
to break into a packet of biscuits,
it seems the current battle of strength
between man and machines
is being waged on a more regular basis,
to the utter frustration of consumers.

I suppose when all is said and done,
we can understand the manufacturers
want to use the latest technology
to package their products efficiently
with security and economy,
but the strength of an average human
is finite so a battle can be prolonged.

It has become more apparent that
even tablets need abnormal pressure
to thumb a dose from the foil,
and reassurance that vacuum sealing
is purely for our ultimate benefit,
is no consolation as your coffee cools
while rummaging for some scissors.

The Business of Success

Have you noticed that when a champion tennis player
is happily holding up a much-coveted trophy,
a following acceptance speech mentions 'the team'
and you may come to the realisation
that behind many of these exceptional individual feats
there is a vast network of support making it possible
to achieve success in this ultra-competitive domain.
Become an icon that ordinary mortals aim to emulate.

There are managers, coaches, dieticians and physios,
accountants tallying travel costs of the entourage.
Unearthing all the multitude of legitimate expenses
to be claimed as tax deductions
from the sponsorship deals honing in for the publicity,
the endless, massively complicated rigmarole
engendered by the guaranteed ongoing popularity
that sports stars can attract after captivating a nation.

We naturally assume that this player in the spotlight
has also won a bucket full of money
and feeling a genuinely happy, personal satisfaction,
but is the relentless training schedule worth it?
The travelling instead of quality time with the family
worth the pressure of others' expectations?
So let's hope the economics don't get so complex
that our idols are left no option but keep competing.

Conviviality

In town, it is a pleasantly sunny, Sunday morning
and the monthly growers market in full swing
with the stalls as usual, doing a roaring trade.
As well as the vegetables fruit, flowers and plants,
the choice of takeaway foods and beverages
from a diverse range of different ethnic origins
is indulging the tastebuds of a burgeoning crowd.

The elderly pushing their walkers cope patiently
with the plethora of family dogs on leashes
who have obviously visited this market before,
so behaving well in anticipation of the stall
that offers all manner of delicious canine treats.
The hand knitted scarves are really popular
and the watercolours attracting a lot of interest.

A baker of homemade bread is serving a queue
near a musician who is playing a modern hit
with several teens taking advantage of the beat.
As usual, the delightfully relaxed atmosphere
helps us to forget current challenges for a while
and is always a more than welcome respite
to see us through the next four weeks to come.

Expectation

Hurray! Spring has now arrived again
with its annual promise of renewal,
days of longer, much sunnier weather
and the joy of more outdoor activity.
Nature's beauty is well on its way
in its resplendent glory
to again invigorate the environment,
put the proverbial spring in our step
and encourage more positive feelings.

The birds are returning from escapes
to more salubrious northern climes
and families settled in their old nests
in my backyard trees.
Lawns are heaving a sigh of relief
and already appearing to be greener.
The lemon tree is awake and in bud,
perfume from freesias ramping up
and the azaleas almost in full bloom.

Disruptive fogs are but a memory
and washing drying on outside lines
but hang on a minute!
Just being walked past the house
are the three rescue greyhounds
who are now living down the street
and still wearing their winter gear
so perhaps in my over excitement,
I have waxed lyrical a tad too early.

Puzzlers

The compilers of modern crossword puzzle books
are obviously an eclectic, sharp-witted bunch
with a great knowledge of their personal worlds
and this is reflected in the diversity of clues
being presented for our anticipated mystification.
But after a while an avid enthusiast may realise
that certain patterns are becoming quite evident
in the content and nature of many of the grids.

Someone has a huge knowledge of religious life
so is a cloistered novice enjoying some privacy?
Another has an understanding of the nobility
so must have a close connection to the peerage.
One pays technical attention to music theory
and is possibly a musician of professional calibre
while an entertainment junkie between shows
names pop groups, films or stars, current or not.

Some words are never uttered in day to day life
being too convoluted for normal conversation
but over time, the addicts remember them
with a triumphant feeling of smug confidence.
Sometimes, the answers are so plainly obvious
our first response is completely dismissed.
Others so ambiguous eliciting hearty disbelief.

But whoever weaves these networks of words
is consistently stretching the brainpower
of all of us hooked on this mental stimulation
and will be forever grateful for their erudition.

Saving the Planet

Front gate recycling
is now the trend,
with assortments
of all kind of items
being presented,
signs confirming
that all of it is free.
Outgrown toys,
kitchen appliances,
old garden tools
or total surprises
can be in the mix
and when passing,
can't help stop
to view the array,
and succumbing
to the enticement
of a zero cost,
choose an item
and take it home,
but if a mistake,
can reposition it
by the letter box,
confident that
somebody else
and environment
can still benefit.

Disaster

Driving home after a trip to the shops,
I pull over to allow a fire engine in full lights and siren
go thundering urgently past,
and immediately feel a pang of selfish concern
for the well-being of my own wooden abode.
I follow in the saviour's wake until my turnoff arrives
and with a heartfelt sigh of relief,
watch it roar onward towards its destination
without me giving a moment's thought
for whoever or whatever is awaiting its arrival.
But after unpacking the shopping and relaxing back
into my familiar and precious home comforts,
I feel so contrite for my insensitivity
for all those involved in the emergency
and trust the situation is now under expert control.

A Little Escape

What a great relief that the news headlines
which lately report more gloom and doom,
have been usurped by the unthinkable.
Five lions had escaped from a zoo enclosure
and while the situation was now resolved,
the sheer novelty of the bizarre occurrence
is a welcome respite from statistics.

It seems that on a primary school excursion
to a Snore and Roar Taronga Zoo experience,
the children plus other overnight campers
were alerted by a code one siren,
advised to leave all their possessions behind
and follow a keeper to a safer location.

For the couple of hours of the emergency,
their teacher kept his pupils busily diverted
until the all clear was sounded
after the father lion shepherded his cubs
towards their own familiar habitat
and zoo staff had assured all concerned
that the integrity of the containment fence
was now being thoroughly examined.

But what a real treat to be discussing this
rather than speculation about the economy
and what an experience for the children
who, with a feeling of lingering pride,
can regale their grandkids all about the day
when they very nearly got eaten!

Inking

On this weekday morning at the shops,
I see through the window that the tattoo parlour
is doing its usual steady business.
Sitting comfortably and relaxed on the lounge,
two women are leafing through a catalogue
then both smiling, point and nod in agreement
while on another,
an elderly man is slowly turning over pages
after giving each one a thorough examination.

The popular modern trend is now quite evident
as warmer weather sees more skin visible
and wonder if these indications of permanency
may be a comfort in an ever changing world
and while I consider this when I am moving on,
begin to speculate
if a simple little smiley face discreetly placed
might be a definite possibility in the future
or as usual, turn out being just a brief fantasy.

Go Team!

Which ever sport you enjoy following,
the same highs and lows seem to arise
regardless of the nature of a contest.
The tension then super-excited buzz
when your team has won by a whisker.
The agony after leading all the way
but pipped at the post by a lucky move.

Someone has been penalised unfairly
if they are a member of your team
but naturally, getting their just deserts
if an opposition player is on a charge.
Any accusation of off-field indiscretion
is always true or no doubt false
depending on your loyalty's direction.

But oh, the delight of relaxing enough
to allow your feelings to run wild,
encouraging your lot or booing theirs.
Reviewing the outcome of a game
with other supporters in the interval
until the next showdown has you
back in your seats, primed for battle.

Whose Town is it?

The local pigeons are a truly brazen lot.
Quite regardless of the vehicular or pedestrian traffic
they go about their daily routines
with an indifference to those who share their domain.
With a confidence
engendered by generations of ancestors living here
before we humans invaded their habitation,
they expertly evade anything perceived as hazardous
to settle along the footpaths outside the stores
as we passing shoppers step around them,
our concern for their welfare obviously greater than
any consideration they have for us.

In sight of the bakery door, they wait for the crumbs
dropped by kids already wolfing down treats,
while on the grassy patch near the bus stop shelter
others sun themselves,
but alert to anyone there enjoying a snack
and more often than not the observation rewarded.
Thankfully we co-exist in an amicable détente
but everyone knows who are really calling the shots
and its not those without feathers.

Distraction

It is a balmy Saturday morning,
and the usual charity sausage sizzle is in full swing
outside the local hardware emporium,
and the aroma of frying sausages and onions
is sometimes much too enticing to resist.
Before you have considered it,
you find yourself with a handful of steaming bun
and munching away in the convivial company
of other fellow gourmands
until finally, scrunched-up paper in the bin,
fingers and mouth wiped, you continue inside,
almost needing to refresh your memory
for the reason why you are here,
ruefully aware that the job you are preparing for
is still awaiting you back home.

Joy

Out of all proportion in a life's history,
one minuscule moment of delight
can engender an unexpected pleasure
that may enhance the rest of the day.
Like sighting the moustache
etched across the nose of a local bus.
Accidentally finding a long-lost sock
and reuniting your favourite pair.
A surprise text proving someone cares
or parking in that last available spot.

Initial sip of your early morning coffee
or first time a child writes his name.
An Ebay purchase is a perfect fit,
or expensive treat a half-price special,
all brightening things up,
and as a warm smile from a stranger
has truly been a raiser of spirits,
I am now determined to reciprocate
and pass one on to someone else,
hoping that they too will feel uplifted.

Commercialism

As always, the current television ads are a broad collection,
but conceding that the sole aim is to engage the viewer,
some are so convoluted their whole purpose is lost
as we struggle to even ascertain the nature of the product.

Circumstances that arise in real life can be so involved
that the actual selling point can disappear in all the detail
and fantasies so complex in style that by the time
the intention is finally revealed any interest may be gone.

But I guess we should be grateful for what we get to view
for without sponsors to finance the whole enterprise,
any commercial television stations could not exist
and our favourite shows just figments of our imagination.

The Hirsute Pursuit

The iconic mullet hairstyle for men
seems to be making a comeback.
From behind, one can no longer be certain
whatever gender we are following
when luxuriant, shoulder-length locks
are being highlighted by the sun.

Appearing more often these days
is a moustache, beard or designer stubble
and a fully shaven male face
becoming less frequent to behold
with guys now rivalling the fairer sex
in conforming to current fashion.

The Gambler

It was a red-hot tip from an acquaintance
whose friendly neighbour had a cousin
who'd done some work at Titan's stable,
and revealed that its jockey had confided
that the horse had a definite chance
of winning its next race.
While having no real interest in the sport,
temptation of some insider information
was much too difficult to resist,
so she finally decided to take the plunge
and wagered a full hundred dollars
on Titan's victory the following weekend.

With an utter lack of racing knowledge,
the odds of twenty to one were fantastic
and in her mind for the next few days,
excitedly spent her winnings,
juggling the possibilities with delight.
Cruise to Tahiti? New washing machine?
Upgrading her ancient mobile phone?
But instead of being first across the line,
Titan had come in second-last
and with her profound disappointment,
vowed any future horse connections
be just Melbourne Cup sweeps as usual.

Garbage

We humans have the tendency to believe
we are the smartest creatures on the planet
but having observed an eye-opening event,
wonder if our assumption is just self-serving.

The usual red- and green-lidded rubbish bins
were lining the kerb awaiting collection
when a passing cockatoo alighted on a red,
seemingly, having had prior experience
with the significance of the colour coding,
and with a carefree, confident abandon,
kicked off the stone that was placed on top,
gave a handle a confident upward thrust
with its versatile beak to dispose of the lid
then disappeared inside to enjoy its repast.

On emerging, it briefly ruffled its feathers,
then leisurely soared into the nearest tree
for some private postprandial grooming,
leaving us rethinking notions of superiority.

Milk

In a period long consigned into history,
milk was delivered by a milkman
directly to all the customers' homes
and ladled from the depths of a churn
into their own billycans or jugs,
still in its original, full cream state.
But in the commercial enlightenment
of our modern world,
supermarkets have rows of alternatives
to suit every taste known to mankind,
each brand's possibilities attractive
to many prospective discerning buyers.

These days, full cream is still favoured
but in addition to traditional skim,
it is now available organic, lactose-free
or without a particular protein,
and all a natural enough progression,
but boldly lined up beside them
there is an almond, oat, rice and soy
also labelled as 'milk'
which, to me, seems a gross misnomer.
Just another illogical sign of the times,
but at least, as in that era gone by,
the containers are now being recycled.

Ouch!

Bindiis have infiltrated the grass again,
tentacles ready and waiting
for bare feet to invade their domain
so woe betide any of us unfortunates
who with soles unprotected,
dash across the lawn to the letter box,
extrication from the thorny villains
worse than is already being inflicted.

Wondering how something so minute
can cause us so much aggravation,
we tiptoe towards the path
vowing to never be so forgetful again,
despite moments of temptation,
but fearing sometime next summer
there will quite likely be a replay
of the same ridiculous performance.

www.ingramcontent.com/pod-product-compliance
Lightning Source LLC
Chambersburg PA
CBHW071036080526
44587CB00015B/2635